How I See It

Abigail Moore

BookLeaf Publishing

Presentation by *BookLeaf Publishing*

Web: www.bookleafpub.com

E-mail: info@bookleafpub.com

ISBN: 978-93-95890-38-0

First edition 2022

ACKNOWLEDGEMENT

A special thank you to Mrs Spring for teaching me to read and spell when I was in her Reception class at Cliff Park Primary School in Gorleston.

The Hair in my Heart

I don't need a hairdryer,
To dry my soaking-wet hair.
My hair is connected to my head,
My head holds within it my brain,
My brain is connected to by beating heart,

...and my heart is as warm as a summer's day

The Bump On My Rump

There's a bite on my bum,
  a bump on my rump

Mr Mosquito came into my room,
  looking for a midnight snack

He must've spotted my peachy bottom,
  flew down and landed

A little chomp, a little nibble
  and now I have a bump on my rump

A Thank You From My Teeth

I brush my teeth and my teeth say
        "Thank-you"
Thank you for keeping me clean,
Thank you for making me white,
    sparkling, pearly

Say "cheese!" so everyone can see the teeth

"Everyone loves us," say my teeth

We're famous now

The Flower

A single flower in my garden
  Always catches my eye

It is pink.
Not bubblegum pink,
Not salmon pink,
It is neon pink.

It stands out because it is so bright,
Standing tall and proud of its boldness,
  In the middle of the flower bed.

It is modest.
The other flowers don't get jealous,
Until I visit that special pink one,
  with my scissors,
  fill a vase,
  and snip its flower stem

Picnic on the Moon

Packed my sandwiches, and my cakes
Then I made a chocolate shake

Got my bag and packed it well,
Planned my route and said "Farewell"

Asked my mum to buy me a rocket,
And off we went to the moon

We're counting down from 10 to 1,
Hear the blast off, then it's done

I pass the clouds into space,
The rocket glides through this starry place

We land safely, with a bump,
Ready for our picnic on the moon

The Socks

The family is moving,
To a new house,

The socks are in the box,
Waiting for a pair to be chosen to wear,

The socks were excited.
The socks were thrilled.
When the box top opened.

The box top opened,
The face appeared,

The socks knew it was time to shine.

But none of them were chosen,
They weren't going to be worn,

The socks were moving again,
Into a drawer,
That they've never seen before.

City Lights

Driving up a hill,
Driving down a hill,

In the city

I see all city lights,
    tiny and bright
Shining like little stars in the sky

Little apartment lights,
    people live there,

Their lights in their own little world.
Every star the centre of a universe.

The Space in my Face

Where are my teeth?
Where have they gone?

Seven weeks ago,
I lost my baby teeth ,
The two in the front,

It's like they're afraid,
To come out and see my mouth

They could be friends
With my other grown up teeth

But for now I'm gappy,
And not very happy,
About the space in my face.

Empty

The Mouse in the House

Grampie is fussing again,
About the mouse in the house,

He sets up the mouse traps every week.
He's tried snap traps, humane traps and poison,
Even peppermint oil,
But there's still a mouse in the house.

We've seen the mouse go up and down to the
basement
He scurries across the kitchen like he owns the
place,
He probably wonders why we're here,
    just like we wonder why he's still here.

He's a clever Mr Mouse

He sees food,
But knows it's a trap
So he passes by the trap,
Into the kitchen

I imagine he opens up the fridge,
To get some cheese

Opens up the cupboard and gets some peanut
butter,
Returns with it to his underground home.

He used to have a family,
   but now more.
They all got caught in Grampie's traps
Now he's single.

He survives because he learned from the
mistakes of the other mice.

What if...?

If tomatoes are fruit,
  is ketchup a smoothie?

Is toast just bread with a suntan?

What is leaves falling down
  are just trees on a diet?

What if juice is just fruit,
  feeling under too much pressure?

What if the rain is just the clouds crying?

If you pee in the sea,
  do you still wet yourself?

Why is it OK to pick your nose,
  and pick your friends,
  but you can't pick your friends' nose?

Go To Your Room!

Go to your room!
Right now!
Go to your room!
For a time out!

My mum CAN be nice,
But sometimes gets frustrated,
When my little brother is being unkind.

...however...
I'm an angel.
See my shiny halo?
See my white, feathery wings?

My sister is in the middle.

Do you think you are an
 Angel,
 Devil,
 ...or in the middle?

The Wedding

Today is a big day.
The groom wears a suit and the bride wears
white,
Today is their wedding day.
She walks down the aisle,
The groom smiles,
Today is an important day.
She's carrying flowers,
Hair and makeup takes hours,
He just got dressed after a short shower,
But today is a special day.
They'll exchange rings,
A soloist sings,
This is a great day.
Before the end, a smoochie smoochie,
Now they're husband and wife,
Happy together for the rest of life,
Today is their wedding day.

Dedicated to Uncle Gavin and Auntie Rowan on
their wedding day, 3rd September 2022

Pillows

Pillows on your bed,
Clouds for your head,
Cotton candy inside a pillowcase.

Dreamland

Mummy bought me a dream catcher,
Hung it in my room,
She said it would catch the bad dreams,
And let the good ones through,

I closed my eyes and drifted into dreamland.

There's cotton candy all around,
And pizza is for free,
You'll never see a bossy man,
Or a crying girl,

Vegetables aren't even a thing.

Everyone has a different dreamland,
This one is all for me,
If your dream catcher took you to dreamland,
What would yours be?

Dinosaurs

Dinosaurs.
Pterodactyl was the one who could fly,
Dinosaurs.
T-Rex was the one with the powerful jaws,
Dinosaurs.
Diplodocus was the one with the really long
neck,
Dinosaurs.
Ankylosaurus was the one with the spikey ball
tail,
Dinosaurs.
Triceratops had three sharp horns on its head,
Dinosaurs.
Stegosaurus had spikes all down his back,
Dinosaurs.

Are all extinct.

Colours

Red
Juicy like a cherry,
Excited like a postbox,
Orange
Sour like grapefruit,
Warning like a traffic cone
Yellow
Soft like a banana,
Scented like a marigold,
Green
Zingy like a lime,
Hopeful like a recycling bin,
Blue
Tiny like a blueberry,
Vast like the sea,
Purple
Spherical like a plum,
Tye dyed like my favourite t-shirt
Colours

Outside/Inside

We're all different,
We're all the same.
We're all different,
We're all the same.
On the outside,
There are differences,
On the inside,
We're all the same.

Hair, eyes, skin, abilities,
You can see how we are different.
But on the inside,
bones give us structure,
muscles help us move,
blood goes through our veins.

We all have a loving heart,
Beating inside of us,
Born to spread love, joy, happiness

Chocolate

Yummy chocolate,
Delicious chocolate,
Minty, sweet, nutty, caramely,
Chocolates

A little nibble,
A little bite,
The chocolate is in my mouth.
My tongue moves it around,
Making it melt,
I swallow it down,
It makes my face and tummy smile

Dear Queen

Dear Queen,
What is is like to be a Queen?
Do you wake up early or late?
Go to bed at midnight or half past eight?
Get to eat for breakfast whatever you want,
whenever you want?

I heard you never carry money,
Is that true?
Then why do you need all those handbags,
To match every dress? Every hat?

Are corgis really the only dogs you like?
What's wrong with a sausage dog? A pit bull?

Everyone loves you,
They line up and cheer,
But do you have real friends,
Who you like to have near?

Now that you're gone,
We're not all that happy,
Thank you for your years of service,
Your Royal Highness,
Your Majesty
Dedicated to the memory of HRH Elizabeth II, on
her passing, 8th September 2022.